Conquering
Panic Attacks

Conquering Panic Attacks

Douglas Kong

Retired Psychiatrist

PARTRIDGE

Library of Congress Control Number: 2016908627
ISBN: Softcover   978-1-4828-6615-5
                 eBook   978-1-4828-6614-8

Print information available on the last page.

To order additional copies of this book, contact
Toll Free 800 101 2657 (Singapore)
Toll Free 1 800 81 7340 (Malaysia)
orders.singapore@partridgepublishing.com

www.partridgepublishing.com/singapore

CONTENTS

CONTENTS

DEDICATION

This book is dedicated to my wife, Margaret for her constant love and encouragement, and to my wonderful children, Adeline and Terence.

ACKNOWLEDGEMENTS

I would like to acknowledge all my former teachers, mentors, colleagues and friends, who contributed one way or the other to the successful completion of this book. Their conversations help shape my ideas as expressed in this book. I also acknowledge all my patients and clients, both past and present. I learnt so much from my time with them. My profound appreciation goes to Marilyn Schoeman, the "Green Light" lady who encouraged me to put my thoughts in this form.

CHAPTER ONE

It Feels Like Dying!
(Panic Attacks Can Be Very Scary)

Panic attacks are horrible. If you have ever experienced panic attacks before, you know that is true. That feeling of palpitations and tightness around the chest, breathlessness and getting out of control, feeling that you are going to collapse and you cannot prevent it. You feel as if everything is spiralling out of control, a need to get out of wherever you are whether in a room, an auditorium or supermarket. And it comes without warning. You can be alone at home doing nothing or outside with friends enjoying a drink, watching a movie, shopping or reading in the library. It just comes like a tidal wave and it sweeps you with it, and then you get all or any combination of the sensations described above.

Because you feel so horrible and you do not quite understand it, once you have experienced a panic attack, you start to get wary of it. You watch out for it coming, you become very careful in case the tidal wave comes again. As you watch out for it warily, you gradually feel tenser and, more stressed. You try to control it when it comes. But when it eventually comes, you realized you really cannot control it. It spirals up, up and up. The sensations you feel, get more intense and become intolerable, and people are not able to help.

So what do you do?

If the feelings are so intense and getting out of control, and you are feeling your chest tightened with feelings of dizziness, going mad and so forth, you really don't have a choice. Fearing for your life and safety, you are likely to rush to the emergency department of the nearest hospital you know. Your life is at stake!

At the emergency Department, you would be given a thorough examination by the attending doctor. Because your heart is beating very fast, you will be given an ECG examination, and perhaps other blood examination for evidence of acute conditions like a heart attack. It is likely that by the time you reached the hospital, the sight of the doctor in his white overall and stethoscope slung around his neck is so reassuring that your panic may be slowly receding, or it may not. If your pulse is still racing and you are obviously still in the midst of the panic attack, you will be given an injection, in your buttocks, or in severe cases the drug will be injected into your vein for a quick response.

Whatever it is, by the time you are given the injection, you would have calmed down and the panic attack is now gone. The good doctor would have assured you that there is nothing wrong with you, only a panic attack is all there is to it. And if you are fearful that it may come again, a medicine will be prescribed for you. You will be told that if the panic attack comes again, you are to take the medication, and then you can go back home. Like many patients, you are grateful that there is nothing wrong with your body.

After the first attack, you are likely to have more attacks. They will vary in intensity and severity. Your response to it will also be different depending on the kind of fears you have. If you are terrified of the panic attacks, and you are getting them frequently or severely, you will likely frequent the hospital each time you experience the attack to get help. And if they are indeed severe enough, each time you will be given an injection for you to calm down. At this point, the doctor will likely refer you to a psychiatrist and you will be given an appointment with the psychiatrist for consultation.

Like most people, you are likely to be nervous during your first consultation with the psychiatrist. Some Asians are afraid of seeing a psychiatrist because they fear madness. They may harbour some superstitious belief that a psychiatrist would pronounce them mad. The result is that they keep postponing their visit to one.

When eventually you get to seek a psychiatrist, it is likely that the severity of the attacks is quite debilitating, and the intensity of the attack is such that when the attack comes, you try to take the medication given to you at the Emergency Unit to break the panic attack. And because it takes about 10-20 minutes for the medication to take effect, you may overdose on the medication because you feel 1 dose is not effective. When eventually the medication takes effect, not only is the panic attack stopped, but you also feel drowsy from the cumulative effect of more than 1 dose. Because of its effectiveness, many patients would rely on medication than try psychological strategies. I would advise that you should ultimately be weaned off from relying on medication to break and to prevent panic attacks.

That will be the natural history of panic attacks for many sufferers who know no better. In fact, the percentage of sufferers receiving medical treatment is very high. The figures for lifetime treatment for panic attack sufferers is 61.1%, while for Panic Disorder with Agoraphobia, the lifetime treatment is 96.1%, so the burden on society of panic attacks and Panic Disorder is very high indeed.

For a small number of sufferers who stumble on the non-medical treatment offered by previous Panic Disorder patients, it is not totally effective as well. These ex-Panic Disorder discovered by trial and error some solution to their panic attacks. Yes, there is no doubt that whatever solution they have discovered, worked for them, but such single solution may not work for everybody with Panic Disorder or panic attacks. There will always be a small or larger proportion of sufferers who will not respond to that one technique.

As a clinician who worked with patients with Panic Disorder and panic attacks, I cannot afford to have my strategies not working. For if a strategy does not work, as an expert, I have to offer another one that will work. Hence over time, I develop a repertoire of strategies that enabled me to treat every Panic Disorder successfully. Thus for my treatment to work, there is one and only one caveat, the patient must be willing and want to follow through with the treatment, only then will it work.

In fact, by conceptualizing Panic Disorder as a disorder of habit, albeit a very bad habit, in my practice, I was able to announce later to every patient with panic attacks coming to see me that Panic Disorder is pre-eminently treatable, I was able to give them hope and motivated them to follow through with the treatment!

The fact that a single technique may not work for all, and the fact that for a single individual, he would be able to find a technique that will work for him is illustrated by this example. When invited to beta-test my video course, this panic attack victim later fed back to me that the most powerful technique in this book and course, was the one that externalize the panic attack. I suppose he is a perfectionist and being able to externalize it removed all the pressure and responsibility for himself, and he was able to consider panic attacks as "not-self" rather than part of himself.

Now offhand, for myself and a lot of other people, we would not consider such a technique to work best for panic attacks. But there you are, and the reason why it worked for him was because of personality variables which I highlighted above.

So, I commend this book to you. I do believe that if you do suffer from Panic Disorder and panic attacks, you will find within these pages something that will truly help you. The video course provides more support material for you to use to help you to more fully implement the techniques described in this book.

Lastly, there is also a support site where I am able to provide psychological support and resources for Panic Disorder and panic attack sufferers. For many victims of panic attacks, such support can be of great value especially when no one seems to be able to understand what they are going through. The provision of such a support site is warranted by my experience of difficult cases of Panic Disorder and panic attacks.

My own view of difficult cases is that they are due either to psychological trauma and a negative mindset with their attendant negative thoughts. My own professional stand is that panic attacks cannot be thoroughly removed from the victims' lives if these are not addressed. One of my patient's very personal description of her treatment with me highlighted it very well, and I like to reproduce the account of her experience here:

I was 16 when I started having regular panic attacks. These attacks escalated and by the time I was 18, they became so frequent that I was unable to step out of my home.

Because of my inability to even get about daily activities, I sank into depression. It was a vicious cycle; the feeling of impending doom suggested heightened anxiety, and the anxiety-fuelled panic attacks pulled me deeper and deeper into depression.

During this time, I had consulted numerous doctors in public hospitals and private clinics. I had never stayed in therapy or been on medication for more than 2 months, as I never felt connected with the doctors. I couldn't feel that they could truly understand what I was going through and I was unable to relate to their way of treatment.

In 2002, at the lowest point of my life, I met Dr Kong. He was a firm figure yet gentle and compassionate. He spent time to understand my condition and did not dismiss any of my concerns regardless of how minute and insignificant they might have been. The sessions I have had with him were meaningful and unlike any other doctors I had seen before, he did not file me up as a classic textbook case of adolescence anxiety. I was respected as an individual, for the first time.

We worked on mindfulness and relaxation techniques. Under Dr Kong's guidance, we confronted my fears and anxiety through exposure therapy where I was to imagine real-life scenarios which frightened me. Gradually, I learnt to cope more effectively with these fears. These techniques were simple enough for me to practise myself at home, or anywhere and anytime it is needed. Naturally, the anxious response within me diminished. Within six months, I was able to function independently and have a regular social life while keeping the panic attacks under control.

Dr Kong was able to give valuable insights on the root of my issues. With his help, I reconciled these differences I have had and slowly my world changed. He had supported me through my transformation and I am very pleased with the treatment I got from him. His effective strategies, coupled with his wittiness and open-mindedness, made the treatment sessions inspiring, wholesome and constructive.

I never needed another doctor.

The above account highlighted the fact that one technique was not enough, for panic attacks is about living, an adjustment to life that requires a complete adaptation on the part of the individual.

It also highlighted the fact that the medical model is never enough, in fact, without psychological treatment, medical treatment is bankrupt. Very early on in my career, I was looking for psychological and social factors in schizophrenia, a very biological disorder in psychiatry. I was impressed by the fact that expressed emotion and family therapy has an important role to play in the relapse and prevention of relapse in schizophrenia.

With this I commend this book to you, for among the wide range of interventions for panic attacks which I shall be introducing to you, I am very confident that one or more of these will be the answer to your problems.

If you need more than the advice offered in this book, you may wish to consider purchasing my video course, and the support site as well. You will find in them the complete answer to all the needs that you are likely to have. Lastly, I can offer life-coaching from me or a member of my team on the internet.

What I cannot offer is medical treatment, or the medical diagnosis of your panic attack. No, not even a second opinion or a medical referral. For that you have to consult a medical professional where you lived. That is certainly beyond the scope of help I am offering.

CHAPTER TWO

How I Got Into The Hunt
(About Me and My Background)

I am a retired psychiatrist. I came into psychiatry because of my interest in psychology and would have taken up psychology as a course of study after my high school, which in Singapore, was then called the Higher School Certificate (equivalent to the British GCE 'A' levels). I was deeply interested in helping people and had served as a church counsellor. My Chemistry teacher at that time had advised that I should pursue psychiatry instead of psychology as far back in the sixties, psychologists as a profession was non-existent in Singapore, and there was no demand for them. So, I enrolled in MED school with an eye to specializing in Psychiatry which I did.

This part of my background is important because it will help you to understand why I look at psychiatric problems with a different set of lenses. By nature, I was nerdy and academically an achiever. Hence, I was very much a loner and felt left out socially, yet I yearned for social interaction. It was in such context that I discovered my inner strength as well as learning techniques to help myself. Among the authors that greatly influenced me in those days, are Dale Carnegie, Norman Vincent Peale, Joel Goldsmith, and Maxwell Maltz. The last was a plastic surgeon who taught in his book, Psycho-Cybernetics, several exercises to relax and to improve our self-image. I practised those exercises with much benefit to myself and later recommended such exercises to patients who would benefit from them. It was such experiences that caused me to be sold on self-help techniques, and I encouraged my patients to be independent by urging them to use similar self-help techniques.

Given this background, you can understand why I am so passionate about psychological treatment and self-help. When I was a medical student, after reading for several hours in the Medical Library, one of the ways I used to relax was by reading some light novels. Occasionally, I would go to the psychology section and read some psychology books. Some of the psychological books which I enjoyed reading were books on psychological treatment, especially those that had to do with psychoanalysis. Thus, I eagerly read books by Guntrip, as well as other books on psychotherapy, such as Melanie Klein, Michael Balint to name a few.

A set of books which I read a few times over was the 6 volume set of Autogenic Therapy by Wolfgang Luthe and Johannes Heinrich Schultz(1969). I was fascinated by the technique and by what the technique was able to accomplish with patients. I eagerly followed the instructions, practised it on myself and later, used it to help patients who needed help with relaxation training and therapy.

Autogenic Therapy is a form of relaxation training that can be used for treating psychosomatic disorders. I used it initially for my own difficulties with sleeping, and later as a psychiatrist, I used it with heart patients, patients with migraine and other psychosomatic disorders including fibromyalgia and irritable bowel syndrome among others. It was certainly a powerful technique. My Chinese patients whom I taught Autogenic Therapy to, showed me the many similarities between Autogenic Training and Chinese Qigong training, and some of them modified the Autogenic technique to be in line with their Qigong practice.

While I was training to be a psychiatrist, I eagerly sought to learn how to do psychotherapy. I eagerly sought for supervision with seniors for psychotherapy with my patients and knocked on the doors of psychologists to learn from them, their techniques of psychological treatment including novel ones such as Personal Construct Therapy among others.

In 2009, I got myself certified as an EMDR therapist. I learned this technique so that I could better help my post-traumatic stress patients. For many years, I had been using hypnosis to help those who suffered from post-traumatic stress.

After inducing them into hypnosis, I would use psychoanalytic techniques to help them to work through the trauma and come to terms with it. The problem with this technique is that when the trauma is severe, it was impossible for patients to recall it without becoming very unstable. EMDR therapy seems to have less of this as a drawback although it can still be an issue. In practice, this means that you got to put EMDR aside temporarily for the moment and use a more structured approach to help them overcome the psychological trauma before doing more supportive and healing work with them.

One of the most important influences in my career was a psychoanalyst by the name of Dr Greenlaw, who provided weekly supervision on a group basis. He was an ardent advocate of group psychotherapy and it was from him that I learned a lot of group work and group techniques. Another notable influence in my life was Dr Michalacoupoulos, a psychoanalyst of Greek extraction. I am not sure I got the spelling of his name right, but he was certainly an erudite person who in group supervisory sessions would theorize about the case we were discussing. These two stalwart gentlemen helped me to formulate my thinking about psychological issues.

Later on in my career, my passion in psychological treatment led me to collaborate with other colleagues to form the Association for Group and Individual Psychotherapy, Singapore in 1997. I had networked internationally as well and was President of the Asian Pacific Association of Psychotherapists (2003-2008), an affiliate of the International Federation of Psychotherapy as well as a Board Member of the International Association for Group Psychotherapy for six years (2004-2009).

CHAPTER THREE

Clarity About Panic Attacks
(What It Is)

How I learned about Panic attacks

My first major exposure to this phenomenon of panic attacks was when I was a Visiting Fellow in the Behavioral Medicine Program at Stanford University back in 1987, I was observing a massive study called the "Upjoin study". This was basically a study of the drug Alprazolam, a tranquilizer that was found to be effective in panic disorder because of its very rapid onset of action. Its effect can be felt within 5 minutes and on an empty stomach, some subjects confirmed that the effect of the drug can be felt within a minute or two. The calm from Alprazolam comes suddenly and for panic attack sufferers, it is always a great relief to see the calmness that you normally know, sets into your body suddenly as the medicine begins to take effect. I had during my training days in London experienced a panic attack, once while crossing the road. And because I knew what it was, I had ignored the panic attack. It did not recur again, and I did not experience any further attack. Hence this research study was of great interest to me.

From time to time, I did help out with the study and had sat in with their research assistants when they were interviewing clients. The research assistants were well trained in interview techniques and were very humane and empathetic in their approach. From them, I picked up some very useful interview skills which I was able to apply them later on in my clinical work.

Soon after my return to Singapore after this stint overseas, I decided to go into private practice, and it was in such a setting that I continually encountered patients with Panic Disorder. Initially, I followed the experience I gained in Stanford by adopting a medication-based approach which worked amazingly well.

However, I soon observed that panic attacks follow a pattern. The first attack can be very mild, although frightening because it is something largely unknown to the patient. The fear come about because of the intense anxiety associated with a panic attack. Over time, the attacks appear to grow in intensity and frequency. This progression had been noticed by researchers, and they termed it "The March of Panic". To a large extent this so-called "March" is brought about by an anticipatory anxiety for the next panic attack. As panic induces a very strong sense of fear, the patient becomes very cautious about the next attack and what it will do to him and his sense of wellbeing.

At its very worse, a patient can be so affected by panic attacks that they become frightened of doing anything for fear of provoking a panic attack. They fear not only doing things, they fear going out of their house because they are not able to handle it when they experience panic attack outdoors. Wherever they may be when they have the attack, they have learned that the best way to handle it is to get home quickly to the safety and familiarity of their home or the hospital's Emergency Department.

Once I noticed this pattern, I began to study how this pattern evolved and how it progresses to the severest end stage. It became obvious to me that the evolution of this pattern involves certain psychological processes which to my logical mind can be reversed. I began to start innovating treatment procedures to help my patients.

I got modest success at first, and then with the advent of neuroscience which basically confirms the validity of what I was doing, I became more confident in treating my patients by teaching this psychological technique while giving them medical treatment.

Understanding of the nature of panic attack took a giant step forward with the advent of the neurosciences which grew by leaps and bounds in the nineties.

With the advent of sophisticated scans that allow us to be able to peer into the brain while various processes are going on and to map out what happens and where it happens, our understanding of what happen when we engaged in mental activities is greatly enhanced.

Thus when we think of something or when talking, for instance, we now know exactly which specific part of a brain centre is being activated by tracking the oxygen utilization of the nerve cells using functional MRI scans. Techniques are also available to trace out the nerve tracks that are involved in brain processes which do help us to understand the specific brain processes that underlie specific mental states and mental experiences. But without going into the myriad details of neuroscience research and findings, I will simply state our understanding of brain processes that occur when you are experiencing a panic attack.

Here goes:

It is understood that panic attack shares very identical characteristics with that of a stress response. The "stress response" is a response to threat or danger when an animal including man, senses or perceives that there is an immediate threat or danger to its survival in the immediate physical environment. This threat for an animal in the wild can be a predator which can effectively kill that animal and have it for dinner. In man, the threat can be anything that threatens his survival as a living person.

The stress response thus triggered, allows us to flee or to fight the threat. This is so because the stress response prepares us to physically face the threat and mobilizes the body's resources to enable us to do so. Essentially the body activates the Sympathetic Nervous System for us to do this.

The Sympathetic Nervous System together with the Parasympathetic Nervous System form what is known as the Autonomic Nervous System. The Autonomic Nervous System as its name implies is not under our voluntary control. You cannot activate either parts of the Autonomic Nervous System, for the two parts of the Autonomic Nervous System, the Sympathetic and the

Parasympathetic, are actually activated by environmental cues of danger and threat picked up by the various senses of the animal concerned. However, by manipulating your experiences, you can actually activate it or modify it in a particular direction You can do this by exposing yourselves to environmental cues that will activate certain emotional states in yourself, or by imagining yourself to be in such a physical state. Thus you can imagine yourself in a frightening situation and you will experience fear and so on.

The Sympathetic Nervous System is, like we say in real life, activated by our sense of impending threat or danger. Sensory input from various sense organs including the eyes, ears and smell of an animal will pick up the sense that a predator is nearby poise to attack. These senses transmit the threat signals to the brain center called the amygdala, buried deep inside within the masses of nerve cells called the emotional brain, or otherwise the old brain which we share in common with more primitive mammals such as the reptiles.

The amygdala is a very interesting part of the brain center. One of its most important function is to scan the environment for threats and danger and then to prepare the body for flight or fight. It senses danger by the signals from the various sense organ which sends impulses to the amygdala as to the status of the environment around the animal. When threat is sensed, the amygdala goes into action. It immediately fires off and triggered a cascade of activity. In turn, the hypothalamus is stimulated which triggers the Hypothalamus Pituitary Axis into action which is the proximal trigger for the Sympathetic Nervous System.

Through the network of sympathetic nerves that go to all parts of the body, the entire body can be stimulated. The nerve endings of such sympathetic nerves secrete a neurotransmitter called Noradrenaline (or Norepinephrine), a very close analogue of Adrenaline(Epinephrine). At the same time, the Adrenal glands, situated just on top of both kidneys, are also stimulated by the Hypothalamus Pituitary Axis and secretes Adrenaline (or Epinephrine). It is the stimulation of the entire body by the catecholamines (Adrenaline and Noradrenaline) from both sympathetic nerve endings and the Adrenal glands that cause you to experience the stress symptoms as we know it. Of course, in the wild, the secretion of such stimulants prepares you to flee or fight the source of threat or danger. In modern life, such stimulation in the absence of a threat or danger is experienced as stress. In panic attacks, because there is no imminent danger all, the excessive stimulation of the body causes you to experience fear and panic.

That panic attacks are nothing more than the stimulation of the stress response by the Amydala is not only confirmed by neuroscience investigation, but when you compare the symptoms of panic attack and that of the stress response, they are virtually identical. The symptoms of a panic attack and that of Sympathetic Nervous System stimulation commonly referred to as arousal are the same. The list of symptoms of both are produced here below:

▶ Comes without warning sometimes with no apparent cause	▶ Feeling of dread
	▶ Fear of dying
	▶ Fear of going mad
▶ Intense anxiety, fear and threat	▶ Ringing in your ear
	▶ Tingling sensation at your fingertips
▶ Palpitation, heart pounding rapidly	
	▶ Dizziness
▶ Shortness of breath	▶ Feeling faint
▶ Sweating	▶ Numbness, pins and needles
▶ Trembling	▶ Shivering
▶ Hot flushes, chills	▶ Shaking
▶ Choking sensation	▶ Stomach churning
▶ Chest pain or discomfort	▶ Urgency – need to go to toilet
▶ Nausea	
▶ Dryness of mouth	

Table 1: Symptoms of a panic attack

As you can see in the above table, except for the first item which is unique to panic attack, the rest of the items in this list of symptoms are also the symptoms for autonomic arousal seen when the Sympathetic Nervous System is activated. So from this table, it is obvious how we can counter the symptoms of a panic attack. If we can induce a state of being whereby the stress response is muted or switched off, we would have succeeded, isn't it?

Panic Attacks and Agoraphobia

Panic attacks may occur with or without the occurrence of Agoraphobia. About a third of panic attacks victim has associated agoraphobia. As its name implies, it is a fear (phobos = fear in Greek). By definition, it is a fear and anxiety of public places and leaving home. The most feared location is where escape to safety by getting out or else to the comfort of home is difficult or embarrassing because of the presence of familiar friends and neighbours, who would otherwise be ignorant of it. To run away when everybody is fine or having a good time seems abnormal and embarrassing.

Agoraphobic attacks occur anywhere and not necessarily in wide open spaces. The places where it can occur include while traveling in a car, train or bus, inside an elevator, being in a crowd, auditorium, theatre or cinema, in a large store or mall, on a bridge or standing in line in a queue. When mild, all the victim needs to do is to get out of the enclosed space. In severe cases the victims really have to get to a safer location, in some cases, only getting home would stop the intense fear.

In severe cases of Agoraphobia, the victim is unable to leave home at all, being housebound because of the panic when they step out. They can only venture out when accompanied by someone else usually a family member.

Agoraphobia complicates panic attacks, but note that Agoraphobia is not a diagnosis of a psychiatric condition.

One of the case histories discussed has associated agoraphobia, see if you can detect which one.

Panic attacks are quite common. Epidemiological study indicates that 22.7% of the general population will have isolated panic attacks at least once in their lifetime, while 0.8% will have isolated panic attacks with Agoraphobia.

Only 5% of the general population will have the psychiatric diagnosis of a Panic Disorder, of which a fifth will have accompanying Agoraphobia. Females are 2 times more affected than males. The age of first onset is usually before 24 years and incidences are usually between 15 to 54 years.

A Panic Disorder is diagnosed when there are repeated panic attacks with significant anticipatory anxiety. An important consideration is that in those with a Panic Disorder, their mental state is adversely affected, and their ability to function effectively as a person is also compromised by the repeated experience of panic attacks. Hence a person with a Panic Disorder requires treatment for them to regain their normal functioning and they are likely to be in treatment for a considerable tie as a result.

Chapter Four
Overcome Panic Attacks
(Practical Steps)

Different victims of panic attack have evolved different strategies to counter the effects of a panic attack. They range from breathing exercises to allow a feeling of calm to overcome the excessive arousal of the panic attack, and to flood their entire experience with a sensation of relaxation. The fact that these different strategies can work, do tell us something – that panic attacks can be controlled by non-medical techniques without resorting to medication. In fact, these strategies of countering panic attacks by non-medical means were discovered by different victims who for one reason or another refused to take medication for their panic attack or who refused to allow themselves to be "addicted" to the use of medication to control their panic attack. (This addiction myth is somewhat untrue, as I will explain later.)

Actually the use of non-medical strategies to counter panic attack is very simple. Once you understand what panic attack is, the way to counter it is easy to figure out. Since panic attack is essentially the activation of the stress response, if we can counter or reverse the stress response, we would have found a way to counter the panic attack. If in fact, we are aware that a panic attack is so triggered, we will not only reverse the effects of the stress response once it is activated, we can also prevent the stress response from being triggered if we can stop it dead in its track before it is even triggered.

In fact, it is possible to do all those I have described above. I have for many years helped a lot of patients to stop their panic attacks either without them suffering at all, or just suffer for a short while only. I do this by helping them

17

understand how the anti-panic agent works and how they can use its properties to prevent them from suffering. I used the medication as a bridge. My ultimate goal with each and every patient is to get them to recover completely from Panic Disorder, and be able to maintain that freedom from panic attack WITHOUT the use of ANY medication, absolutely! So here in this chapter, I will teach you a fast method using medication, and a slow method using psychological techniques. The slow method is in the long-term desirable, as one would not want to be taking medication for the rest of one's life, especially when another method of achieving what we want is available.

The "fast" method:

If you are choosing medication or fastest method to break your panic attacks, in order for it to be effective you need to understand the action of the medication you are taking, the purpose and objectives it will achieve, and how you should consume it. So, for the purpose of breaking a panic attack, the medication of choice is Alprazolam, usually called Xanax. Other forms are available which are generic with different names, so you have to look at their chemical name to confirm if it is Alprazolam. Alprazolam or whatever proprietary name your medication carries comes in usually 0.25mg, 0.5mg or 1mg strength. It is very important that you use the lowest effective strength to break your own panic attacks if you want to avoid side effects, notably drowsiness, and if you do not want to be "addicted". Often the problem is not "addiction" but one of dependence on the use of medication to solve the problem of panic attacks instead of taking charge of one's own life.

Alprazolam is classified as a tranquilizer and belongs to the same group as other tranquilizers collectively known as benzodiazepines, which include the widely known Valium (chemical name diazepam) as well as others used widely such as Ativan (chemical name lorazepam). Tranquilizers are anxiolytics which are known as powerful agents for dissolving anxiety by their action on the nervous system. They are very safe, and easily tolerated and certainly better than other groups of medication used for combatting anxiety. They also have relatively low side-effects and the side-effects are usually the result of over sedation due to an over excessive intake of the tranquilizers concerned. Their activity over time also vary. Valium is long active – over 24 hours, while Ativan is 8 to 12 hours of active action, and Alprazolam has only about 4 to 6 hours of activity.

In the last 10 to 20 years, there has been a lot of concern about tranquilizers causing dependence. The risk though is very low. Studies indicated people who abuse benzodiazepines are likely to be abusers of alcohol, and substances such as heroin. However, although the potential for abuse among normal people are low, there is still a lot of concern that people are being exposed to a potential source of addiction. Hence, the use of benzodiazepines has been quite severely curtailed and is now recommended to be prescribed for only a short period of time.

By using the drug Alprazolam as recommended here conforms to this principle of prescription for a short period and more importantly to be used only when necessary. Hence, my advice to all my patients is to stop using benzodiazepines including Alprazolam when they do not need it. And that is why learning the behavioral and other psychological strategies for controlling panic attacks is so very important because doctors no longer willing to prescribe tranquilizers for long term use.

How do you determine your lowest dose of Alprazolam for your body? Start with the lowest dose. Does it have an effect at all? The action of the drug is such that your panic attack and/or associated anxiety should completely disappear. If it does not completely disappear, the dose is likely to be inadequate. To confirm that this is the lowest effective dose, increase the dose, and the increased dose should give you greater effectiveness. If the increased dose gives you greater benefit without any other side-effects, then this increased dose is the lowest effective dose. If the increased dose gives you side-effects, but no added benefits, then the lowest effective dose is your earlier dose. Your increase dose is excessive when you start to experience side effects such as drowsiness, lack of coordination, inability to concentrate, a tendency to fall, and unable to maintain stability on your feet. Immediately reduce the dose back to the lower dose.

So, using this technique, my experience is that for most Asians who are of smaller built, the lowest dose can be 0.25mg and in some cases even 0.125mg (half a tablet of 0.25mg). While for Caucasians and similar individuals with larger frame, it may be higher at 0.5mg. Each and every person is different however, as even with the larger frame body of Caucasians, I had come across one person whose lowest effective dose was 0.25mg.

Therefore, once you establish the lowest dose possible, use this dose to break your panic attack. But when should you take it? You can take it when you are in the middle of a panic attack, and your panic attack should subside within 2 to 5 minutes when you consume it on an empty stomach. If you are familiar with your own panic attacks, you can take it when you feel it coming on and you would be able to prevent experiencing a panic attack entirely.

Obviously, if you are to be able to take the medication whenever you need to, your medication must be near at hand almost all of the time. So, you would be advised to have at least a few tablets of medication nearby or at hand almost all of the time every day. This is not a problem if you are at home, but when you are outside the home or travelling, I would advise that you should have the tablets in your pocket, in your wallet or purse, or else in a bag or pouch which you are carrying with you.

The inevitable question you would ask is: "What if it does not work?" Almost all the time, I would say 99% of the time, this would work once you have determined the lowest effective dose. Although, I admit, there are certain situations when you may have to take a second dose to break a panic attack. If you need to take a second dose to break the panic attack, wait for a little while first to ensure that your first dose has already taken effect. As mentioned earlier, the medication takes at least 2 to 5 minutes to act, so taking a second dose too quickly will mean dosing yourself twice and cause you to have side effects after the second dose.

One of my patients who used to get a panic attack whenever he has to board an airplane to fly, and thus stop flying for work or holidays altogether, has an experience that is worth telling. He developed this reaction of fear and panic attacks when he is on an aeroplane after an episode when he experienced terrible anxiety and a mild panic attack during a very bad turbulence while inside the plane. This episode made him very fearful of the plane having turbulences and after that each time the plane experiences turbulence, he would be anxious enough to have a panic attack, and before long, he would get a panic attack with each experience of turbulence. The panic attacks got more severe with each added episode until he was even afraid of thinking of boarding an aircraft. That was how he was when he first consulted me.

After a lot of psychological support and help in controlling his panic attack, he felt ready to confront it on a flight once again. As he experienced mild panic, he started taking his Alprazolam, it did control his panic, and as there was a lot of anticipation that the panic attack would come again, he ended taking a second and third tablet.

He ended up without any panic attack subsequently, but feeling very drowsy, unsteady and groggy as a result of taking too many tablets of Alprazolam. This proved that 3 doses were too much for his very bad panic attack, and in all likelihood, a second dose was all that he needed. A word of advice here is needed. Do not take the second dose until at least 1 hour, preferably after an hour and a half to two hours. This is to allow time for the effect of the medication to be felt.

I do not advocate the consumption of tranquilizers and Alprazolam included, on a regular basis, such as once or twice a day, up to whatever frequency a day, unless you have been diagnosed as having a Generalized Anxiety Disorder. If so diagnosed, you should only consume it on a regular basis under the direction of your psychiatrist and you should tail down the frequency of consumption and stop it altogether once you get your anxiety under control. This should be done in close consultation with your psychiatrist, psychologist or medical doctor that is supervising your drug treatment.

The slow method:

The slow method requires preparation. You need to practice the psychological technique to be conversant with it, and the more you practise, the more effective it would be for you. The centerpiece of this method is a relaxation training technique. There are many relaxation training techniques available which you can learn. For me, I usually teach the **Autogenic Training technique** which is very powerful and can be used for a variety of purposes, but for controlling panic attacks, a less rigorous and simpler technique can be used.

The technique that can be used for our purpose of controlling panic attacks and can be used as well for various purposes including increasing focus and attention, involves a large breathing component. This technique is attached to this book as an appendix towards the end. This technique which you can learn to control panic attack is called the **Quick Coherence Technique**. (Purchase my course, Conquering Panic Attacks, and you get a free recording of both the Quick Coherence Technique as well as the Autogenic Training technique)

You should practise the relaxation technique you have chosen when you are calm, for at least a week or so, before you attempt to use it for controlling panic attack. You can, and some will, try to do it without any practice, to control a panic attack. However, you may face some problems. First of all, you will find yourself unfamiliar with the technique and fumble your way through, or you may find it ineffective. Once that happened, you will lose confidence in it, and rob the technique of its efficacy because you will associate negative thoughts with the technique. Practice comes first before using it. Use it like a tool, and be conversant with it so that you can use it effectively and powerfully.

At the same time, begin to focus on the kind of self-talk statements which you will use to encourage yourself to gain control of the panic attack.

Self-talk or the internal dialogue of your mental life, provides the emotional flavour of your conscious life. They provide the opinions and evaluations made by yourselves on your experiences of the external world. If you are self-aware, you will realize that this self-talk is going on all the time in your head, providing you with an evaluation of the external world. When your internal dialogue is negative, critical, suspicious or paranoid, you see the outside world as inhospitable and dangerous, and your emotional level of tension and anxiety rises. Conversely, if your self-talk is positive and supportive, you are likely to feel good about yourself. This internal dialogue does not sometimes reflect reality but is often a reflection of your hopes and fears. Obviously such a system of internal dialogue is useful for you to focus on danger in the environment when needed or else to use your attention for useful work and meaningful reflection when you are in a safe environment.

Can you change your internal dialogue? Yes, you can, especially when these opinions and evaluations are at variance with the reality as we know it. A negative evaluation may have arisen as a result of an actual dangerous situation, but the brain then constantly evaluate subsequent other similar situations as fearful and negative, although such subsequent experiences may not at all be dangerous and should not cause you any anxiety or fear. In such circumstances, by changing the negative self-talk to a positive and supportive one, you can reduce a lot of stress for yourself.

In the context of panic attacks, the first experience of it may have been fearful and dangerous, but later experiences of panic attack may arise because provocations from environmental cues which may recall the very first episode, but which are non-dangerous at all. Hence although you may have a panic attack, the panic is in fact not warranted, and that's how the panic attack because of these constant recurrences become a very bad habit.

The accompanying internal dialogue is often negative and fearful causing you to anticipate the next panic attack with fear. Now you can understand why the next panic attack will come sooner and more severe with each panic attack being experienced. So, if you change your internal dialogue and self-talk, you can begin to calm down. And once you start to calm down, you can gradually get the panic attacks to be under controlled, simply by switching on an emotional tone in your mental life to be more supportive and positive.

In the appendix, there are examples of self-statements that you can use to control the emotional tone of your psychological experience so that panic attacks are not triggered off. Again as for relaxation technique, practice repeating these self-statements which are positive/neutral and supportive, so that they can replace your spontaneous negative self-statements. In fact, to begin with, you should memorize these positive self-statements so that they can gradually become second nature for you.

In order that the appropriate self-statements can be used powerfully to counter the negative self-statements, I have divided the experience of panic attacks into phases, so that you can assign the correct self-statements to each phase of your panic attack experience. In the Appendix referred to earlier, you will find the self-statements are assigned to the 3 phases of the panic attack experiences which I have identified. The earlier you can get your body to calm down, the less severe will your panic attack will be. Hence learn the self-statements for the first Phase, when you feel the panic rising. The more you can control your panic attack here, the more will your confidence in yourself rise, and your panic attack will be controlled easily and rapidly. My video course pays a lot of attention to details of changing the self-statements in a panic attack, because it is so critical to get your body to get the panic attack under control!

Once you have mastered the technique and the self-talk statements, you are ready to confront any panic attack even without medication by following the procedure outlined below:

1. Panic attack often comes with a lot of anxiety. So you have to reverse the anxiety using a relaxation technique. Therefore, you need to put yourself in a situation where you can effectively allow yourself to relax quite effectively. To do this, look for a place where you can at least sit down. This can be anywhere close by. In Singapore, where toilets are often clean and well maintained, isolating yourself in a toilet may well be a good solution. Otherwise, some place for you to be able to calm down will help tremendously. This is obviously not a problem at home where you can easily find a place to sit or lie down.

2. Talk to the panic attack like as if it is some living thing existing outside of you. Give it a name, this can be any name, the name of someone you like or dislike, or an adjective such as horrible, terrible, wicked or the Bad One. Talk to it like, "I know you, N (name)", "There you come again, N", "You are not welcomed, N", "I will keep you under control,

N", "Get out of my life, N" or similar such self-talk sentences. You will find that by externalizing it, you can control it better. Trying to control something which is a part of yourself is much more difficult.

3. Next practise the Quick Coherence technique by first taking a few deep breaths. Do deep breathing for up to 5 times. Do not breathe deeply for more than 7 times.

4. Depending on the stage of the panic attack you are in, repeat the self-talk statements to help you maintain your calm and to keep it under control. If the panic attack is rising: use the appropriate statements for it, and at the stage where the panic attack has peaked, again use the appropriate statement as well.

5. After the panic attack is over. This is the most important part of the psychological technique to make it even more effective when you next encounter it. In this step, review the experience of the panic attack that you have just gotten through with. How did you do? If a grade of 10 means that you have complete control of the panic attack and 7-8, is when you experience very mild panic, while a grade of 0 is where the panic attack has dominated your experience as it takes over you, how would you grade your ability to counter the panic? Whatever your grading is, make use of self-statements to get it under control, so that your mastery of the panic attack can rise to 8, 9 or even 10. Constantly make use of self-talk statements to support and bolster your confidence and help you to strengthen your defences the next time another panic attack come upon you.

6) This last step is important and takes place in between the panic attacks. This is *not* an optional step even when you have contained the panic attack successfully. This is because in my view, panic attack is associated with some form of psychological trauma, except when your bodily constitution is of the sensitive type and your panic attack is provoked by some chemical stimulation by the ingestion of chemicals such as caffeine or nicotine.

Psychological trauma must be dealt with by attending to the negative thoughts and painful memories associated with the psychological trauma and with the onset of panic attacks. Besides psychological trauma, there may be limiting beliefs imposed on us by our experience with authority figures and influential peers in our lives.

These limiting beliefs and accompanying thoughts prevent us from achieving and attaining success in our lives, and we condemn ourselves to a life of mundane mediocrity and second best achievements. Such limiting thoughts can be a sufficient basis for our disinclination to want to conquer panic attacks and may be compounded by other problems that we may have including existing psychiatric and medical problems that we may be struggling with.

Deal with all these other associated problems if you seriously want to control and conquer panic attacks.

So there you are, you have the 6 Step Solution outlined above which you can use to counter and eventually conquer panic attack in your life.

It is my experience that a Panic Disorder is one of the most treatable conditions in Psychiatry. I have thought of it as a habit disorder. It is a bad habit which is thrown up by a traumatic episode in one's past, or else formed from negative thoughts from one's experiences in life. The reaction of the stress response may well be the appropriate response at the time of the original trauma, but now that it is over, it is no longer useful.

The original trauma because of its threatening danger caused us to overlearn the response that we have as we go through the pain of the panic attack. And because the response was a survival instinct, that's why we still respond to it even though the danger and threat is no longer there. It is a bad habit.

Ditto with negative thoughts and limiting beliefs

Negative thoughts may be appropriate and a defensive action on our part in the past at the very first triggering episode or experience. But now such thoughts and beliefs are no longer useful, for we do not have to defend ourselves against anything in the current situation that is provocative. Instead, these thoughts and beliefs are now in the way of being able to achieve more for us to make progress and succeed in our lives. Hence, they have to go, but like bad habits, they are hard to get rid of, and this topic is taken up in the next chapter.

CHAPTER FIVE

Eradicate Negative Thoughts
(Instil Positive Ones)

The last chapter ended with some comments on negative thoughts. In this chapter, I will give you a better understanding of what negative thoughts are. You will know the power of negative thoughts once you start to have panic attacks.

When you have your first panic attack, and you experience all those terrible and unpleasant feelings and sensation in your body, it is not only unpleasant, it is very terrifying. You do not like these terrifying and unpleasant feelings and sensations, because these are associated with something bad happening to you. These feelings include the following such as: you going out of control, going mad, collapsing, about to have a heart attack, about to faint and about to die. No, you do not want to have these feelings and sensations and together they make you feel uncertain as to whether your very own physical existence is in question. Its extreme terror for you.

You do not like these feelings/sensations because they portend something terrible is about to happen to you. In this context, you start to have negative thoughts about your panic attack. Will it happen again, will you survive it, or are you actually going to collapse, die or have a heart attack or one of those terrible end states that you are frighten of.

Of course, negative thoughts protect you, by making you conscious of what can possibly go wrong and your very survival is threatened. The survival value of negative thoughts in the wild, cannot be underestimated and perhaps you may not call them negative thoughts either.

For in a situation that is unsafe, negative thoughts protect you from danger. Thus a tiny mouse seeing a piece of cheese may be tempted to eat it. If he does, he is trapped by the mousetrap and he dies. But if the tiny mouse is cautious and avoid that cheese or watch another mouse go at it first, he would have save his life.

Many things in life for each one of us, are similar to the cheese in the mousetrap for the mouse. These things, which we desire, are either an opportunity or it may be dangerous for us. Like the mouse, if we rush forward to embrace it, we may be trapped into a very dangerous situations and sometimes avoiding it may well preserve our life and our safety. That's how negative thoughts may have a protective value for us.

But in modern life, and in situations where we are with friends and loved ones, negative thoughts by raising the spectre of danger and threat all the time, may cause us not to be able to enjoy the fun and fellowship of people who seek our good as much as we ourselves. When this happens, negative thoughts are truly negative thoughts and they become a barrier for us to move forward to whatever desirable outcome that may be ahead.

Life itself is truly complex, and I acknowledge that even in such situations there may be danger. For trust can be broken, and love can be betrayed. When that happens, danger and threat looms large. Your negative thoughts are justified. But betrayal and broken trust are unusual in such contexts and body language may give a hint of what is to come, if we read it accurately and act on it that is.

Assuming that life is normally without threat as in normal modern living, panic attacks because of the unpleasant sensations they provoke will give rise to negative thoughts. "I am going to have a heart attack", "I am going to die", "something is wrong with my body" and so on. And these are the negative thoughts that will make us take action and rush to the emergency department of a hospital, any hospital.

The trouble is, negative thoughts induce fear in us. They provoke our physiological arousal, and this arousal in fact, will lower the threshold for possible panic attacks in the future. Thus, negative thoughts can lead us to have another panic attack which may aggravate the severity of the negative thoughts in us. The diagram below depicts this accurately:

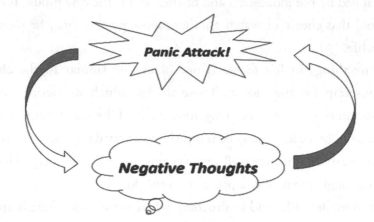

Figure 1: Relationship between Negative Thoughts and Panic Attacks

Given the kind of circular relationship between negative thoughts and panic attacks, it is no surprise why panic attacks keep escalating in patients and get steadily worse until you seek for help. It also explains why dealing with the panic attacks alone is not enough, you need to tackle the root cause(s) as well as contributory causes such as negative thoughts.

Experts have tried to classify negative thoughts in an attempt to understand them. Below are some categories of negative thoughts which may be useful to you to understand the thrust of your negative thoughts and hopefully will help you to identify them more easily in your thought life.

Here are some examples of types of negative thoughts

▶ Pessimistic generalization: "I did not finish the project on time, I never do things right"; "If something good happens in my life, I usually pay for it with something bad"

▶ Filtering (Negative abstraction): "My boss says it's great, but he also said that I made mistakes, he must think I am hopeless"; "if I worry enough about my problems, I will feel better"

▶ All or Nothing Thinking: "I made so many mistakes, I am hopeless"; I have to do things perfectly, otherwise I am a failure"

▶ Blaming self: "If someone is upset, it's definitely my fault"; "It's obvious she does not like me, otherwise she would've say hello"

▶ Negative Self-Labelling: "I feel like a failure, therefore I must be a failure"; "If people knew the real me, they wouldn't like me"

▶ Catastrophising: "I cannot perform well, I'll never succeed"; "I forgot to turn the iron off, it will burn the house down"

▶ Should/must statements: "I shouldn't get upset at all"; "People must be good and nice to me at all times"

▶ Mind reading: "I can tell that people don't like me from the way they behave"; "They must be talking about me as they seems to be looking this way"

▶ Magnify negative, disqualify positive: "Life feels like one big disappointment all the time", or "he's angry with me for what I had done, he will not want to see me ever again"

▶ Truth of emotional reasoning: we believe that what we feel is automatically true. "I keep getting headaches, something must be wrong with my brain"

▶ Fallacy of change: People need to change because our hope of happiness depends on them. "if only my mum can change, I am sure to get better"

The direct effect of negative thoughts on you is that they make you feel upset, irritated and frustrated. In the long term, they can make you depressed and the effect on your body, as a result of depression, is the suppression of your immune system, leading to physical disease. Hence, it is of utmost importance that you need really have to tackle this problem of negative that aggravate your panic attacks which in turn aggravate your negative thoughts.

You can now see that being able to stop your panic attacks is not enough, you need to stop and stamp out the negative thoughts you are having, that constantly fuel and feed the next panic attack that is to come. Not to deal with negative thoughts is to invite panic attacks back all over again.

So use the description of the different types of negative thoughts to help yourself identify the specific negative thoughts you are having. Discuss it with your psychiatrist or whichever therapist you are working with to ensure that you are comprehensive enough when you identify your negative thoughts so that it is complete.

How to challenge negative thoughts

The traditional way of challenging negative thoughts is to consider the irrational part of the negative thoughts by questioning it, probing it to show it is illogical and then replace it with positive thoughts. Neuroscience research however, seems to indicate that the process of considering negative thoughts does strengthen negative thoughts. That's because when you consider a negative thought, you are activating the negative thought pathway thereby strengthening it. Neuroscience has also mapped out the pathways of negative and positive thoughts.

Because negative thoughts have a protective value as far as our survival is concerned, the pathway for negative thoughts from the forebrain to the stress center, the Amygdala (responsible for our response to threats an danger) is direct, immediate and rapid. In contrast, the pathway for positive thoughts, called the regulatory pathway, is routed through the Anterior Cingulate Cortex and interrupted by at least one synapse, a nerve to nerve interface. This slows down the conduction. This is because positive and regulatory thoughts are conscious rather than immediate.

Based on the findings of neuroscience, it makes sense to stop the negative thoughts by actually saying "Stop!" consciously to yourself to terminate the negative thought. Then what you do is to consider the opposite corresponding positive thought, and rehearsing it repeatedly using as many body actions as you can and involving more than one sense modality. This is reinforcing the positive thoughts. For example, if your negative thought is about your failure to do something, a positive thought such as "I can do better the next time." can be repeated with action/movement so that different sensations of the sound of the words, the way you feel it articulated and the way you feel the movement of your hands, legs and body. Involving the body in this way deepens the memory. The more sensation/movement is associated with this thought, the better it will be captured in a network of circuits, and the better it will be remembered.

So when the panic attack strikes with the negative thoughts, because you have rehearsed the positive thoughts, you can recall the positive thoughts with much less effort. If the positive thought is entrenched in your mind and consciousness, you will find that that will influence your panic attacks, making them less and less likely because the positive thought would have a calming effect on you thus negating a very important trigger for the panic attack to come.

This is how confronting the negative thoughts can impact your panic attack positively.

If your negative thoughts are persistent and strong, you may need to seek therapy or help to sort out the contributory causes of your negative thoughts. Among the experiences that can lead to negative thoughts are unsupportive parenting from early childhood, experiences of being abused or bullied, grief and losses, and psychological trauma. All such experiences cause you to feel angry against the perpetuators of such experiences and cause you to be suspicious and paranoid about people. Accumulation of such experiences eventually lead to feelings of loss and depression.

In summary, the steps to take in dealing with negative thoughts include:

1) Identify the negative thoughts,
2) Write down the positive thoughts that can confront and overcome it,
3) Rehearse your positive thoughts,
4) Use the positive thoughts when you experience the negative thoughts,
5) Deal with past events and trauma that may be fuelling your negative thoughts.

CHAPTER SIX

Snapshot of Success
(Case Studies)

My patients with Panic attacks

#1 One of my very first patients was a man called Julian(not his real name), who came to me with panic attacks escalating in severity and frequency. His panic attacks were such that they restricted his own personal freedom as well as interfered with his job as a Civil Servant in a ministry concerned with public health. After he was treated with medication, he was well controlled, but declined to learn psychological techniques to conquer panic attacks because they "take too much effort". He would see me about 2 or 3 times a year to get a supply of Alprazolam. His use of the medication was much less than the prescribed dose though, and that's because his panic attacks was as stated, well controlled. His panic attacks were much less frequent and he used his medication only when he started to feel a panic attack coming.

Over time, I discovered that what actually happened was that he was taking Alprazolam whenever he was anxious. That's because he did not feel at all confident to handle any anxiety or panic symptoms and so taking the medication was a kind of short cut for him. He was quite happy "depending" on Alprazolam to handle his anxiety and panics. Note that this was not a chemical or physical dependence, but a psychological dependence because of his lack of confidence in himself being able to overcome it on his own.

About 6 years after he was on medication, he met a lady and fell in love with her. As his relationship with her deepened, he began to think of marriage and starting a family. Suddenly, he became motivated to want to live a life free from panic attacks and medication. He wanted to recover completely now and trade his fears for a completely new life without medication. And so he made a special appointment with me and announced that he wanted to eventually stopped his Alprazolam one day. He readily booked sessions with me to learn whatever psychological techniques I could teach him for him to accomplish that. We then embarked on a course of training him to practise relaxation training and to use it to conquer his panic attacks. Within 6 months of training, he was completely free from panic attacks, and used frequent relaxation exercises to keep himself calm and free from anxiety. He still faced his work stress though, but he was coping better and learning to enjoy his work.

#2 Mrs Ti, a housewife was housebound with a very severe case of panic attack, when her husband called me urgently one day to request me to make a house call to attend to her because of her severe panic. After hearing her story, I told her husband that if she wanted to live and be free from her symptoms she should come to my clinic instead. This was because if I were to go to her house because of her anxiety, this would simply reinforce the anxiety and worsened it in the long run. The husband understood and persuaded her to come. At my clinic when I met her, I congratulated her success for being able to leave home and come to the clinic for treatment and proceeded to help her.

Her devoted daughter a secretary felt bad about her mum's illness and expressed her desire to care for her mum to the point of remaining single all her life if necessary. It turned out that mum was having panic attacks because she was fearful of being alone. She had been a housewife all these years bringing up and caring for her children, and when one of her son got married and moved out to stay, she was forced to consider that eventually all her children would no longer be around and she would be alone with her husband. In fact, at the time of her panic attack, all her 3 sons were all married and staying out, leaving the youngest daughter being the last to go. She must have insisted that she needed her daughter and entreated her not to get married and leave home.

(Eventually we had to work on her relationship with her husband because of the way they were relating).

It was in this vein that the daughter made her vow to care for her mother. She was uneducated and simple, but in-spite of that she was taught deep breathing to help the older lady to relax, but a large part of treatment was social.

I showed her daughter that marrying was probably the best decision she could made for her mother, because if she did get married, her mother will be blessed with a son-in-law and grandchildren, and her life would be even happier. For the old lady, I tried to get her out of the house and be active socially. She started attending church and began to socialize among the senior ladies as well as play card game with friends and neighbours. Her daughter eventually got a boyfriend and got married.

A couple of years later, her first son was born. The grandmother was delighted and offered to care for her grandchild. She was also involved in church activities at about this time. She had been free from panic attacks but was afraid of stopping medication. I encouraged her to do so, and encouraged her to use her breathing exercise as a means of gaining confidence. I told her that if she was happy, the panic attack would never return. She trusted me and within a month or so, she had stopped medication and her panic attacks never return.

#3 Chek Kwang, a small business owner suffered from very bad panic attacks that prevented him from travelling and meeting his business clients and associates abroad. It turned out that there were a lot of worries in his life. His younger brother was in university and he worried about whether he had enough funds to see him through to graduation which was another 18 months to go. His mother has been unwell since the death of his father and now had kidney problems that required frequent medical check-up. And he was solely responsible for bringing her to the hospital for check-ups in between his work schedules.

His wife was struggling with his ADHD son and her part time work. All these worries make him anxious about his panic attacks. He was concerned that his panic attacks were affecting his ability to bring in income through his business. So, by the time he reached my clinic, he was in a severe anxiety state besides having panic attacks.

Since his panic and anxiety were quite severe, he was put on medical treatment to stabilize him. Concurrently, I taught him relaxation techniques and he was able to use it to somewhat control his anxiety. Then one day, he told me that he had to meet an important client in Hong Kong. Sensing an opportunity to get his panic attacks under control, I encouraged him to use the trip to confront his panic attacks. He was prepared psychologically to counter the panic attacks which was still severe at this stage. I pointed out that besides psychological techniques; he still had medication to break any panic attack should the psychological techniques proved not to be as effective as it should be. Armed with these thoughts and sufficient medication, he went on this trip.

On his return, he reported that the trip was good apart from the flight there and back. On the flight there, he was filled with anxiety and kept feeling that a panic attack would come any time. He ended up taking quite a few doses of tranquilizers. In fact, he reasoned, considering the fact that he was so anxious, he might as well take enough tranquilizers and go to sleep than to face it. On the return trip he fared better, not least due to the fact that he achieved his business objectives. He took just one tranquilizer and was able to enjoy some inflight entertainment.

As advised by me, he used a glass of wine to help him calm down as well. After this major confrontation with his panic, Chek Kwang's confidence improved, and he became more courageous in confronting his panic attacks. Within a matter of months, his panic attacks not only reduced in intensity, but he was completely off tranquilizers. It took him slightly longer to come off antidepressants as he had some problems shoring up his confidence because of his numerous problems. He was off medication some 6 months before his brother's graduation, and continued to see me for quite a while for psychological support for another 9 months or so.

#4 Shirley was a young adult when she came to see me. Her father had died when she was a teenager and her mum and mum's lived-in-boyfriend had frequent quarrels. In such circumstances, her panic attacks began, and it got progressively worse to the point where she needed hospitalization. While in hospital, her mother spent a lot of time with her. Before her discharge, her mother decided to split with her boyfriend and this helped to reduce her anxiety and in time her condition improved. Over time, she improved significantly and was able to be taken off medication. However, she was still having recurrent panic attacks at odd times.

She was taught breathing exercises as well as other anxiety relieving techniques. She engaged in psychotherapy and her issues of grief and trauma over her past were worked through. One feature of her attacks was that it occurred when she was with people, and during the attacks, her friends would rally round her and she would cling to them, and they would keep talking with her. My observation was that it was the social support of her friends who kept talking to her when she was having her panic attacks that helped her to calm down eventually and the attack to subside. In fact, on more than one occasion, it was her friend who called me to ask as to what should they be doing to help her contain her panic attacks.

....

The above stories of my patients were all rather severe cases of panic attacks. But they were able to achieve complete recovery from their panic attacks. There are more patients who suffered from very mild forms of panic disorders and panic attacks. Some only saw me once, mainly for reassurance and support. Others were prescribed tranquilizers to be taken when they have panic attacks or when it was coming, while they were taught psychological techniques.

Some of them, in fact never used the medication at all. I had one patient who hardly used any tranquilizers, but who would come every year for his prescription of tranquilizers. He kept these medications in a special pouch he carried in his pocket with him everywhere he goes.

It seemed that the thought that he had medication on standby if he had a panic attack was enough to keep him calm and confident. Eventually, he was persuaded to learn some psychological strategies to bolster his skill and confidence and increase his sense of freedom from panic attacks. In fact, he learned a simple technique of relaxation which was more than sufficient to shore up his confidence and kept anxiety and panic attacks at bay for almost all the time. It was that simple.

So, if you are suffering from the horrors and pains of panic attacks, you would like to be like the people I have helped, to conquer panic attacks completely in your life. You would want to be completely free from panic attack and live a life of freedom, meaning and purpose. You want to be able to live the life you choose based on your circumstances. You do not want your life to be restricted and limited just because of some anxiety and panic attacks.

All the four individuals whose stories appeared above have had their lives handicapped and curtailed because of their panic attacks. But when they learned how to reverse the psychological processes by which panic attack increase in severity, they were able to reverse the "March of Panic", roll back the experience of anxiety and panic and learn how to live panic free lives.

Such skills can be learned by almost all ordinary persons who suffer from panic attacks. And if you do suffer from panic attacks, learning these skills can help you to completely eliminate panic attacks from your life. This is particularly so, if you are motivated to be free from panic attacks without the use of medications.

For I have a few patients whose panic attacks had been completely eliminated by the use of medication. They were stable and generally free from panic attacks, although panic and anxiety symptoms do occur rarely from time to time. They cope with the anxiety and impending panic by taking a small tranquilizer dose. These attacks of anxiety and impending panic, don't occur very often and they do not consume tranquilizers on a daily basis, more usually perhaps once or twice a week or much less than that. When I teach them psychological techniques to overcome their anxiety and panic, they were not motivated to learn them, preferring to depend on medication from time to time.

If you are not motivated to learn the technique, there is nothing much I can do for you. You have to realize though that you have made that choice yourself. The outcome will be different if you make a different choice.

Another reason why these psychological techniques may not help is the fact that you may be having one of the many medical or psychiatric conditions associated with panic attacks. If so, proper medical evaluation and diagnosis, followed by targeted intervention can help you overcome panic attacks completely as well as deal with the correct medical and/or psychiatric conditions that cause your panic like symptoms in the first instance.

So when you sign up for my course on **"Conquering panic attacks"**, you will get my step-by-step instruction on how you can get the panic attack under control in your life, and then to completely conquer it by eliminating it from in your life. You will learn how to tackle and remove the various panic attack associated conditions which aggravate the severity of your panic attacks.

This course only teaches you the psychological and related techniques to deal with panic attacks and its associated symptoms. I do not use any medication to control your panic attacks. If you are currently on a prescribed medication for your panic attacks, you may want to discontinue your medication once you are free from panic attacks and you have gained confidence in using these techniques without the support of medication. Any discontinuation of medication should be done under medical supervision as there may be side-effects when you are doing so. And you have a strong case for discontinuing medication if you are indeed free from panic attacks for a few months.

So sign up for my course, the panic attack course which will teach you the skills that will enable you to live a life free from panics. To ensure that you benefit from this course fully, if you purchase my course, you shall be entitled to lifelong email support from me or a professional member of my team. Please also note that my team and myself do not provide you with prescription drugs to treat your panic attacks. For that, you have to consult a medical professional in the place where you live. We are also unable to recommend any medical professional that practice in your locality as we would be totally unfamiliar with the practitioners in your region. What we can do is to help you with self-help techniques, provide you with support, including social support for you to try and practise it, and to make recommendations as to other choices you may wish to consider including consulting a medical expert and consultant.

Please note that subscription to this course is not a substitute for psychiatric consultation or treatment. That's because panic attacks can be associated with medical and/or psychiatric conditions, and if you have a medical or psychiatric condition, this has to be treated otherwise there will be complications arising therefrom.

If you are currently consulting a psychiatrist or consuming medication under medical supervision, you should not discontinue such medication without first discussing this with your attending doctor. Should you for any reason is unhappy with your medical attendant, you have every right to seek for a second opinion, although this will be totally outside the purview of our assistance to you.

If you have never consulted a medical professional, you should consult one, so that you are certain that you are suffering from a Panic Disorder which is a disorder of recurring panic attacks, and not some other medical or psychiatric condition which would require proper and adequate treatment.

CHAPTER SEVEN

Final Perspectives
(Panic Attack In Context)

We have come to the end of this book on Conquering Panic Attacks, and writing this book has been for me an exercise in putting what I have been practising for so many years into a form that is not just accessible to my patients but to all who has suffered and continue to suffer, as well as to those who will fall victim to panic attacks in the future. I feel a sense of satisfaction in completing this book and in the accompanying video course that is now on sale.

I wish you will have the same satisfaction as you overcome the Panic Disorder that you may be having and the panic attacks which you are experiencing. In this chapter I wish to outline the philosophy that undergirds my practice when I was actively practising and how I manage to help my patients attain the freedom from psychological handicaps.

I believe as a practising Christian that it is God's will for all of us to be living a healthy, meaningful and purposeful life: no one should be devoid of satisfaction and happiness. By healthy, I mean that it is our God-given purpose that we should be psychologically and physically healthy. Where disease and illness affect us, we learn to overcome it by learning to live within the limitations of whatever disease that afflicts us and then thrive.

We can learn to enjoy whatever reasonable amount of happiness and satisfaction that we can have and make our lives useful and meaningful. Meaning and purpose is something that we can attain as we engage ourselves in economic activity or in activities that contribute to others in the community out there, including the environment and in relationships.

Even if you do not believe in God, you would find such an ideal noble and acceptable, and draws its roots from liberal and humanistic ideals which all of us can subscribe to, whatever our philosophical and religious orientation.

However, having such ideals does not in any way make us soft, cushy and a pushover.

To survive, we have to be tough and resourceful. Otherwise, we will succumb to the various stresses in life which will come from our vulnerabilities, and lose out to the competition from the environment, and eventually be snuffed out by predators and enemies that for whatever reason would want us not to survive. It is because of such mishaps in our background, and challenges that will always be present no matter where we are, that cause us to be traumatized so easily when things go wrong or did not go the way we wanted, and we have to pay the price of enduring such insults and misadventures.

This trauma, physical or psychological is a necessary part of our development. They will leave scars, and we either have to learn from our experience or else succumb to our weaknesses and be a victim and be destroyed in some way by the threats that confront us or our fears of them. It is such toughness that will enable us to survive and to have that better quality of life that is the substance of the vision I have outlined.

Thus, stress management is not about relaxing. To manage stress is to toughen ourselves so that we learn when not to take on the challenge, and to keep training ourselves to take on more and more challenges and be able to perform in the optimal zone as highlighted in the diagram below.

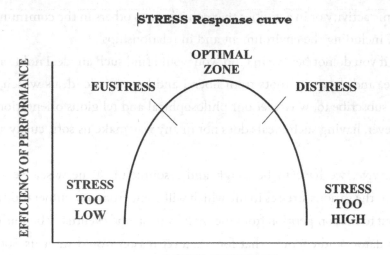

Figure 2: The Stress performance curve

Remember, the stress that is perceived by each one of us is always subjective. The same pressure can give in different individuals and on different occasions, a different perception of our stress levels, for if you are weak, you will certainly perceive more stress than if you are strong. So the ultimate aim of stress management is not to relax more, or be excused (in reality, you cannot be excused from life, can you?), but to train ourselves to be tough and resilient, so that we can deal with stress more effectively by maintaining or improving our performance with enhanced productivity and to be able to bounce back when the stress is over.

So the focus of stress management is the question of whether our performance will be affected. The desired outcome is that we are able to maintain our ability to perform and when the stress is over, to bounce back to our normal selves again. That is toughness and resilience.

If there a limit to our ability to cope with increasing stress? Of course, there is. This limit is imposed by our physical constitution and the limitation of our physiological function and ability. We may able to stretch this to some degree within limits by training. But however, the key to good stress management is to live within our limits really by managing the environment, including our own internal psychological and physiological environment. Anybody who has learnt to perform under stressful conditions know that to be able to perform well under those circumstances know what preparations are needed from habits of sleep to those of diet, and what behaviors have got to be managed so that they will be at their best when the time comes for them to perform. So, another important tenet of stress management is to live within our limits.

It is my contention that Panic Disorder and its associated panic attacks belong to the group of conditions that is the result of a vulnerable period of our life when we face some physical and/or psychological trauma.

The panic attacks are a sort of a psychological scar, which we can deal with successfully if we are to regain our resilience and once again to be able to live a life of fullness of meaning and purpose. And we can, you included, conquer panic attacks in your life successfully.

In short, a Panic Disorder is a condition that we do not have to suffer if we order our lives correctly and we learn to make choices within our limitations. This book and the accompanying video course, is a statement of how we can remove this psychological scar completely from our lives.

Appendix I:

The Quick Coherence Technique^R

The coherence technique^R focuses on the heart as the organ that regulator of emotions. HeartMath Institute called this "heart intelligence" harnessing the ability of the heart to calm down and to regulate the response of the body to negative emotions.

You probably know what it feels like to have a broken heart. In the same way, you will also know what is it like when you are in love and how your heart feels. You know too, what your feelings are when your heart is pounding, from fear, tension or anxiety. From this perspective, your heart is the most powerful organ in your body. For example, you may like to know that your heart can produce an electrical field 100 times greater than the brain and as well as induce a magnetic field 5000 times greater. Every emotion that you feel is experienced first through your heart, with a signal being sent to the brain. When your heart is in a state of alignment, you are in a state that is called 'heart coherence'.

Quick Coherence° is the technique that is especially useful when you start to feel negative emotions such as frustration, irritation, anxiety or stress. Using Quick Coherence at the onset of less intense negative emotions can keep them from escalating into something worse. This technique is especially useful after you've had an emotional storm following a crisis, quarrel or disagreement to bring yourself back into balance quickly.

The heart is a primary generator of rhythm in your body, influencing brain processes that control your nervous system, cognitive function and emotion. More coherent heart rhythms facilitate brain function, allowing you

47

to have easier access to your higher intelligence so you can improve your focus, creativity, intuition and higher-level decision-making. When you are in heart-rhythm coherence, you will be able to perform at your best.

You can do the Quick Coherence Technique anytime, anywhere without anyone around you knowing that you are in fact doing so. In less than a minute, it has the ability to create positive changes in your heart rhythms, sending power signals to the brain that can improve how you are feeling. You can do this within a minute and using this one-minute technique first thing in the morning, before or during phone calls, before an important and stressful meeting, in the middle of a difficult conversation, when you feel overwhelmed or pressured, or when you feel a panic attack is coming or anytime you simply just want to increase your coherence. Just practice the Coherence Technique. You can also use Quick Coherence whenever you need more coordination, speed and fluidity in your reactions.

The Coherence Technique is particularly powerful when used in conjunction with tools that provide biofeedback information. Such tools are easily available, and you may wish to get a simple gadget for yourself.

Here's how you can practice the Coherence Technique:

Before you start on the Coherence Exercise, get yourself into a comfortable position, seated or lying down. Breathe normally and begin to do diaphragmatic breathing. Diaphragmatic breathing is when you breathe in, your abdominal muscles are pushed out, and when you breathe out, the abdomen and stomach muscles fall back into position again.

Step 1: Heart Focus. Focus your attention on the area around your heart, the area in the center of your chest. When you first learn the Technique, it helps if you place your hand in the center and left of the chest where your heart is. Focus your attention on your heart beating. Allow yourself to calm down.

Step 2: Heart Breathing. Breathe deeply, using diaphragmatic breathing, for 5 to 7 times and then go back to a normal rhythm. Go back to deep diaphragmatic breathing for 5 to 7 times again. Focus on your heart, and calm down. Scan your body and relax. As your body calms down, notice any tension in any muscle of your body and relax, starting with your head, and working downwards to your neck, your shoulders, your arms, your chest, your back, your abdomen, lower abdomen and your legs.

Step 3: Heart Feeling. As you maintain your heart focus and heart breathing, activate a positive feeling within you. To generate positive feeling, recall a time and place that brings back happy memories or feel the love you have for someone significant in your life. Feel a warm feeling accompanying this happy, positive feeling radiating from your heart, and reaching to every part of your body.

You can continue by going through the 3 steps and repeat the Heart Focus, Heart Breathing and Heart Feeling all over again or you can terminate this at some convenient point. You will feel invigorated and fresh to do whatever you need to do after a few minutes of creating positive changes in your heart rhythm.

APPENDIX II:

Modified Autogenic Training Protocol

Notes on Autogenic Training: Autogenic training is a technique of relaxation based on the balance of the sympathetic and parasympathetic systems. It was invented by Johannes Heinrich Schultz, a German Psychiatrist in 1932.

The technique taught here has been used by me to help patients for more than 20 years and I have changed it in some ways to suit my purpose.

It is a technique that can induce quite deep relaxation and I have used this technique to treat various psychological and medical conditions where stress is a major factor in the evolution and maintenance of the illness.

I have also used this technique as a basis for self-hypnosis and guided imagery. The latter is most useful in many instances of anxiety associated physical symptoms, the so-called psychosomatic illnesses where you need to institute behavioural change.

You will notice that in the script, some statements are in quotation marks. These are the statements that you should repeat to yourself when you have mastered the technique and are the essential backbone of this technique. The rest of the script is an elaboration of the bare structure of this powerful relaxation technique which guides you as to what to do.

If you need to build in a lot more intervention besides just relaxation because of the presence of psychosomatic symptoms, autogenic training is the best foundational technique to use. For that, you will need some expert help and guidance. Contact a psychologist or a mental health professional for this. Unless you are using this technique for headaches, the last step, step 11, may be omitted.

Now for the technique itself.

1. Find a quiet place where you can be free from distractions. You may lie on the bed, floor or on a mat or else recline yourself in a chair or sofa where you can relax and let go. Loosen any tight clothing and remove glasses or contacts, as well as any ornaments or personal effects that may distract you by their sensations on your skin. Allow your hands to rest on your lap, or by your side or on the arms of the chair. Uncross your legs.

2. Take a few slow even breaths. If you have not already, spend a few minutes practicing diaphragmatic breathing. This is breathing with the abdomen. To do this, breathe in and push your stomach out as you do so, and when you breathe out, allow your stomach muscles to fall back in place.

3. Say to yourself, silently or under your breathe: "I am calm and relaxed." Empty your mind of whatever thoughts you may have, focus your attention on the sensations you can feel on your body, head, back, hands and legs. Be aware of sensations you can hear from around you as you remain quiet.

4. Focus attention on your right arm. Quietly say to yourself and slowly repeat to yourself this statement about 4-6 times, "My right arm is heavy" followed by this statement, "I am calm and relaxed." You can achieved this by imagining the heaviness coming upon your right arm and a sinking sensation as your arm sink into the material on which it is resting on.

5. Focus on your left arm. Repeat to yourself 4 to 6 times. "My left arm is heavy followed by "I am calm and relaxed". Feel the heaviness now in both hands. You may induce a sensation of heaviness gradually going from your right arms upwards to your right elbow and right shoulder, then progressing to your left shoulder, then to your left elbow and down to your left arm until it reaches your left hand.

6. Say to yourself: "Both my arms are heavy" and "I am calm and relaxed."

7. Refocus attention on your right arm again, and repeat to yourself quietly or under your breath "My right arm is warm" followed by this statement: "I am calm and relaxed." You can achieve this warmness by imagining that blood is rushing into right arm from the rest of your body. Or you can imagine that there is a heat or candle under your right hand giving heat and warmth to your arm.

8. Now bring the warm sensation to your chest and stomach and say to yourself: "My chest is warm" followed by "I am calm and relaxed" about 4-6 times. Feel the warmth like an invisible sheet of warm blanket covering your chest. Bring the warmth to over your stomach region and say "My abdomen is warm" followed by "I am calm and relaxed". As you feel the warmness over your stomach, let the diaphragmatic breathing that you are practising becomes heavier and with a warm sensation.

9. The heavy and warm sensation that you induce earlier on will slow down your breathing. So say to yourself: "My breathing is calm and regular" followed by "I am calm and relaxed" about 4-6 times.

10. You will feel so much calmer that you can feel your heart beat slowing down. Now say to yourself "My heart is strong and regular" followed by "I am calm and relaxed" about 4 to 6 times. Feel the strong beat of your heart slowing down, and direct it to a slower heart beat as much as you can by intensifying the feeling of relaxation.

11. Feel a cool sensation over your forehead. Say to yourself: "My forehead is cool" followed by "I am calm and relaxed" about 4-6 times. When you are able to do this, you would have achieved a fairly deep level of relaxation. Enjoy this deep relaxation for as long as you like.

12. When you have achieved sufficient relaxation and are ready to stop the relaxation, say to yourself: "My arms are strong, my breathing is deep, open my eyes." You do this by gripping and releasing your fingers and allow your arms to regain their strength. Take control of your breathing and breathe deeply a few times, and as you feel more alert, open your eyes.

APPENDIX III:

Self Statements for Use During A Panic Attack

Phase 1: Rising Sensation of Panic
- Calling it by name and talk to it
- My panic attack cannot harm/kill me
- It's my body that has trigger these sensations
- These sensations are just a bad habit only
- I will go through this attack and win
- I will learn better ways of handling this
- I am winning by not being affected by it

Phase 2: At the Peak of Panic
- Nothing will ever happen to me (physically)
- This sensation will soon be over (very fast)
- It is only my body reacting
- I will still be here and well (after the panic)
- The high tide of panic is coming in
- The high tide of panic will go away
- I will be all right, I will not go mad, collapse, or die
- I can go through this and enjoy it

Phase 3: The resolution Phase of Panic
- There you are, it is going away as expected
- I have gone through it successfully, I am still here
- I will learn to "enjoy" my next panic attack

- I have not been frightened of it
- I am still alive and nothing is wrong with me
- I will learn and cope better next
- I am getting better at coping with it
- I will win over my panic attacks